MEASURING THE DISTANCE

flash fiction by

Robert Scotellaro

BLUE LIGHT PRESS ◆ 1ST WORLD PUBLISHING

1ST WORLD
PUBLISHING

SAN FRANCISCO ◆ FAIRFIELD ◆ DELHI

MEASURING THE DISTANCE

1ST WORLD LIBRARY
106 South Court Street
Fairfield, Iowa 52556
www.1stworldpublishing.com

BLUE LIGHT PRESS
www.bluelightpress.com
Email: bluelightpress@aol.com

BOOK & COVER DESIGN
Melanie Gendron

COVER ART
by Achille Beltrame
Permission granted from The Everett Collection

AUTHOR PHOTO
Diana Scott

FIRST EDITION

Library of Congress Control Number: 2012943311

ISBN 9781421886503

ACKNOWLEDGMENTS

Grateful acknowledgment is made to the following publications in which these works or earlier versions of them previously appeared:

6S Vol. 3: "Uncle Sal"
971 Menu: "3-D", "Uncle L"
Apollo's Lyre: "Book of Facts"
Bare Root Review: "Dark Dining"
bent pin: "The Saint of Redirection"
Bull: "Sweet Tooth"
Defenestration: "The Saint of Redirection"
Dogzplot: "Dirty Eyeballs", "Family Secret"
Eclectic Flash Literary Journal: "The Limits of Art"
Fast Forward (a collection of flash fiction) Vol. 2:
      "Book of Facts"
Fast Forward (a collection of flash fiction) Vol. 3:
      "Mr. Nasty"
Fast Forward (a collection of flash fiction) Vol. 4:
      "Fun House", "The Ghost Gets a Visit"
Fiction at Work: "Slugs", "More of the Same",
      "Behemoths in the Basement"
Fiction at Work Biannual Report Anthology: "Slugs"
Flash: The International Short-Short Story Magazine:
      "Stuffed", "Accessories"
Gargoyle Magazine: "Measuring the Distance"
Ghoti: "Goin' Country", "Measuring the Distance"
Lit Snack: "Revelation at IHOP"
Long Story Short: "Strings", "One Better Than the Next",
      "Hawaiian Shirt"
Pen Pricks: "Grandly Awesome"
Postcard Shorts: "Bite-Sized"
Ragazine: "Jacked Up"

Storyscape Journal: "How Joey Z. Saved Us All"
The Best of Eclectic Flash: 2010: "The Limits of Art"
The Linnet's Wings: "Crooners in the Web"
Vine Leaves Literary Journal: "Skyped",
      "Uncategorized Omen"
Willows Wept Review: "After the Earthquake"

Several of the stories in this collection have previously appeared in the chapbook: *The Night Sings A Cappella* (Big Table Publishing).

Special thanks to Diane Frank—poet, teacher, friend.

to Diana and Katie—
for the light they bring

CONTENTS

Sweet Tooth

"You can keep the frogs," my ex says. "But I want all the hand-painted stuff from Italy."

She's brought a list, is sitting across from me in a Chinese hole-in-the-wall, inexplicably named the *Sincere Café*. It's a dive we frequented before she moved out—moved up in the world. She's ticking off items—her pen hovering like a baton.

No, she hasn't dumped me for another man, left me whimpering in her wake wrapped in an old army blanket. It was a high-powered industrialist name Rita—heir to a dozen or so tire plants. She's loaded.

My ex has picked all the peanuts from her Kung Pow Chicken and gathered them in a neat little row.

"That's not much of a concession, Jen," I say. She'd always hated the frogs, probably the only thing she and my mom had in common. The frogs are real (Mexican, I think)—stuffed and lacquered, stretched out comically. They played bongos and tiny red accordions, rode motorcycles and shot pool. They were my father's. My mom hid them behind a jungle of house plants. When he left them to me, Jenny banished them to a dark corner in the closet.

"You sure you don't want them?" I offer. "Rita Rubbermaid might find them adorable."

"I told you not to call her that," she hisses, and to emphasize the point, wags her pen at me.

"Okay," I say, and as I lift a forkful of Ginger Beef—I notice, over her shoulder, the cook raging toward a table behind us. He is a slight man with a grease-stained apron and a nasty look. He reaches under the apron and pulls out a revolver; waves it at a homeless man seated in front of a cup of coffee. The man's face is dirty and his hands are smudged black and he's wearing an overcoat many sizes too large, with only his finger tips showing.

The cook says something to him in broken English; the gun inches from his face, and the man stands.

"I'm not going through the music. You can have the CDs." She smiles, pleased with the scope of her benevolence. Her lips are impeccably painted. She's oblivious to the drama played out behind her.

"Thanks," I tell her.

The homeless man (I've seen him before on the street, panhandling) reaches in a pocket of his great overcoat. He scoops out handfuls of sugar and piles them on the table. The cook flicks the gun toward the other pocket and I notice the three empty sugar dispensers on the table. Wonder what in the world he wanted with all that sugar. Then imagine him lying in a doorway on a cold night, with only a piece of cardboard for a mattress, dipping into those deep pockets with a wet finger and finding something sweet. I wonder what his story is. Everybody has one. Roaming the streets unwashed, alone and penniless, wasn't something you planned for yourself.

The man empties the other pocket. There are two snowy piles now—one trickling down onto the floor. How many degrees of separation are there between any of us? I think. How many blows?

"You need a shave," my ex points out, as the homeless man ambles toward the door—the cook in tow, ranting loudly now in Cantonese.

"I know," I say.

The exiled homeless man leaves behind a foul, lingering odor. My ex turns, pinches her nostrils. "Chrissake," she says.

I pour sugar into a small cup; the dispenser's silvery

flap tipping open till the hot tea spills over, scalding, but I don't flinch—won't give her the satisfaction.

She glances at my cup, my hand. "Why don't you have a little tea with your sugar," she says. I look up at her; her new hairstyle, her smart suit. Those red lips, slightly parted—never lovelier, never more remote.

"Sweet tooth," I tell her.

Bookends

I'd just jotted down an idea for a poem when the two pit bulls bolted from the bushes. One positioned its snout against my rear and the other deep into my groin. They looked like small sharks with feet. I stopped, forgetting how to breathe.

I was in a park I'd often driven past but had never been to before. It seemed a good place for a walk.

"Who you with?" a voice said.

When I turned to look, the dogs dug in deeper, snarling.

"Don't move, asshole, less you wanna go from a *he* to a *she*."

"Whoa. . ."

"I'll ask you again—who you with?"

"Just me," I said.

"You a wise-ass?"

"Sorry," I told him, without knowing what I was apologizing for. He stepped in front of me, a full head shorter with a nasty twist to his mouth, his head tilted to one side. He wore a red hoodie and pointed to my chest. His pits seemed content enough bookending the slim volume I'd become.

"Your colors," he said, "you're sporting your colors."

"This?" I followed his eyes, pointed to the top of my running suit.

"Don't play with me, man."

Confusion merged with panic. It was an awful mix. "This shirt?" I asked, tugging at the material.

"Thems CLD colors," he said. "Don't play dumb, sucka'."

"You mean like a gang? I'm not in a gang. I'm a poet."

"Faggot," he said.

My running suit was getting saliva-basted and I simultaneously anticipated unbearable pain and sudden loss.

"You don't wear blue in this park," he said. He did some kind of hand gestures, curling his wrists and forming his fingers into a distinct pattern and shot them in front of my face.

"But it's not blue," I told him.

"That's blue," he insisted.

"Actually it's kind of green. But I can see how it might look blue in this light."

He had a thin V-shaped goatee which he scratched with one finger.

I was hoping his dogs wouldn't attempt anything impromptu. He reached in his back pocket and removed a narrow paint chip book and fanned it out. "You gonna be missing some parts if you bullshitting me."

"Green," I repeated with a little voice.

He held a panel of graduated hues against my running top.

"You mind if I look?" I asked, peering down. He grunted.

"Sassy Grass," I said. "Well, sort of between Sassy Grass and Kryptonite Green."

"Humm," he said, holding the sample against my chest. "You just mighta hit the jackpot, sucka'." He twisted his fingers up into that configuration again, which seemed to mean so much to him, flashing it in front of my eyes. Then he said something in a foreign language or a slang I couldn't understand, and the dogs relented—flanked him as he walked back through the bushes.

I stood there for a moment with the sun on me, as though I were defrosting, with the word *Kryptonite* knocking around in my head, thinking: Go figure, some fake element from an imagined world just saved me.

Revelation at IHOP

The wife sees Jesus in her pancakes at IHOP. The dark pan marks, distinct—unmistakable. There is even a berry bleeding where the heart should be.

"Is there something wrong?" her husband asks, as she stares down at the plate. Their sons are blowing straw wrappers at each other—banging knees under the table. "Quit it!" one of them says. "Screw you," says the other.

The wife, gazing down, *knows* it is a sign—blowback from that time with the guy who cleaned the rugs. The delivery men who lugged in the fridge—the three of them filling that king size bed.

"No," she reassures. "Nothing." The husband watches as the syrup she pours spills over the sides. Her fork cutting into a sandaled foot, up an ankle—along His holy robe. "Good," she mutters, her mouth fuller than he's ever seen it.

"Simmer down," the husband chides, swatting at a son without looking. Her fork reaching for the center now—chopping out a juicy red heart. "Umm," she says. "Yum."

Tuxedo Epiphany

He awoke not knowing why, but with a clear and certain knowledge that he must purchase half a dozen tuxedos and, regardless of weather or circumstance, alternate wearing them.

At *Java Junction* he straightened his bowtie and flicked lint from his shoulder as he met with a woman he'd been seeing.

"What good is life if you can't shake things up a bit?" he said.

"Christ," she told him, glancing around, hoping she didn't see anyone they knew. "You're dressed like a goddamn penguin. And for a week now in bed, just unzipping. Not taking that damn thing off. Any of it. And what's with that hat? You look like that ditsy guy on the Monopoly box."

"Yeah, well tell me it wasn't totally outstanding and this penguin didn't know some moves." She gazed at what bloomed, grinning, from that starched collar, got up and never looked back.

He found tennis to be a challenge and beach volleyball, but he was acclimating nicely and the furtive glances and whispers were welcomed *blips* on the screen, in contrast to what was otherwise flatline. When he played one-on-one at the park, he began drawing onlookers. He'd always been a hoop hound in high school and now began frequenting inner city playgrounds and garnering street cred and the moniker: *The Dapper Dude*. His 3-point shot was unstoppable, and his bowtie never on crooked.

He got a job at a rotisserie chicken stand, avoided donning the customary apron, and still managed not getting a single spot of grease on him, as he cleaver-chopped them up for the long lines of customers; basking in their low thrum as they waited.

He even earned a write-up in the local paper with the tagline: CHICKEN CHOPPER, A SHOW-STOPPER! In time he penned a memoir, a Kindle edition on Amazon called, *My Life as a Penguin*.

He was working on a sequel when he met Laura. She had no such epiphany nor desired any, but fully appreciated his small celebrity and their curious adventures in the bedroom. They married and when they grew old, she spent her time filling scrapbooks, dutifully straightening his bowties whenever he came in from the surf and tilting his top hats, just so.

Meg's Reach

Meg is in our bedroom playing *Purple Haze* on bagpipes. That's Meg. Always trying to be different. You should see her—those pretty cheeks bulged out as she blows into that thing. Meg's got dreams so big they could buckle the walls.

Me, Carlos and Frank are watching the Super Bowl. It's the first time in a bunch of years we've got a shot at it. We're psyched.

"Turn it up," Frank says. "And quit hogging the chips." I rip open the bag and spread them out on the coffee table. Meg said she wanted to learn *Tangled Up in Blue*, and a bunch of other stuff, and play Carnegie Hall some day. She's unstoppable when she gets a thing in her head. "Keep practicing," I tell her. "You're an original." Then I watch her huffin' and puffin' and suddenly can't think straight.

I work with Frank and Carlos down at *Get-A-Grip Hardware*. I'm their boss. But for now we're on equal footing. "Shit!" "Damn!" "Fuck!" we all say when our guy misses one my grandmother could've made. When Meg hits an off note, Frank gets up and goes over to Meg's fish tank and reaches a bear paw in and traps one of her Fancy Platys and eats it whole along with a handful of chips.

"Hey, Dickhead," I tell him, "knock it off!" When he sits back down, I let him know he's a real piece of work. He drinks up.

"You're a fucking mutant," Carlos screeches and starts up with that hyena laugh of his. Our guy scores a touchdown and we go ballistic, high-fiving and bottle-clinking. Puffed up like roosters. Like the turf was under our own heels. Like we did it ourselves.

During halftime, three sheets to the wind, I turn off

the volume. We're all clammed up and passing a huge doobie—the good shit, and listening to Meg. Even Frank, with his mouth swung open and tapping his foot.

Hell, she ain't half bad.

Twelve Collapsing Faces

I didn't know what Dad did, but Mom screamed at him with the door closed and I heard her say "That bitch" a lot.

When Halloween came she was still pissed. She stayed up all night scooping out and carving twelve pumpkins and placed them throughout the house. Every one was different, but what was the same was, they all were scary with jagged teeth and crooked chopped out noses and Mom lit candles in them soon as it got dark. Getting up to pee at night was like walking through a haunted house.

Mom's yelling quieted down some after that. But when Dad mentioned getting rid of them a week later, Mom looked up at him from her scrambled eggs and he never mentioned it again.

After a while the creepy faces started to pucker up all wrinkly like angry men and got furry inside. But Mom would still fire them up till yellow light shot out of their eyes, not seeming to care that the tops were caving in and they were beginning to sizzle and turn black inside.

Dad wasn't so busy anymore like he used to be and came home from work the same time every night and brought flowers and other stuff. Mom got a new car, even though the one she had was still good, and used it to go clothes shopping at the mall every chance she could.

By this time the pumpkins were all twisted up and shrunken with their eyes nearly closed like some of those boxers Dad and me watched on TV, and those pointy teeth were poking into each other and bent all which way.

Then one day, Mom just tossed them in the compost and let the ants and flies have them. And it kind of freaked me out to see all those creepy faces piled together whenever

I went out back to play with Pepper. But Mom said, just think how they were going to feed the roses and the other flowers some day and make them so nice and bright. And that's just what happened. Only it took way, way too long before it did.

3-D

He stands outside her door with his cane and a bag of guilt. He knows she's in there because he heard the TV on before he knocked and then it suddenly went quiet.

"It's me," he says. "Look, I'm sorry if I did anything, you know, to make you feel. . . *strange* in any way."

It stays quiet. And he wonders if she's looking at him through the peephole.

A week ago she'd invited him in with his dime store items and he knew, right off, she was different. Not sappy like so many of the others, handing out cash at the door or leading him in by the arm for tea and lonely talk.

"The couch is to the left," she'd said. "Watch you don't bump into the coffee table." She sat beside him; a hint of gin on her breath and the clean, damp scent of freshly shampooed hair.

"Whatcha got?"

He gauged from her voice she was probably in her forties, maybe younger. But it was always hard to tell. He reached in the shopping bag and took out a small plastic microscope, two different sized magnifying glasses and (his best seller), a colorful cardboard kaleidoscope, and placed them on the coffee table.

"Kids love 'em." It was his hook. Everyone either had a kid or knew someone who did. He wondered about her.

"Wow," she said, and he knew what she'd picked, was holding to the light. "How much for the kaleidoscope?"

"Three bucks," he told her.

"And the magnifying glasses?"

"Buck each. Five all together."

He heard her unsnap a purse. She slipped a bill in his pocket and pushed it down deep. He heard the microscope tumble back into the bag.

"You sell much of this stuff?"

"I do okay."

She edged closer. "An accident?" She gently touched one of several deep scars on his face. It startled him. He stiffened.

"I'm sorry," she said and pulled back.

"It's all right. Iraq—a souvenir."

"Fucking war," she said. He found her hand and squeezed it. It was a little clammy. She leaned toward him, her hair brushing his arm.

He started to speak. She said, "Don't say anything."

He released her hand and she ran it back over his face, tracing each long gash, following one down nearly to his lips. He put a hand on her waist—it wandered. She was wearing a nightgown, soft worn cotton with nothing underneath. When he reached to touch her face, she grabbed his hand. "No," she whispered. He slid it back down.

She began gently kissing each scar in a path to his lips. But he needed to know what she looked like. He reached his hand up again to touch her face. Nearly did. But this time she slapped it away, hard, and pulled back. He felt the sofa cushion decompress as she stood.

"What?" he asked.

"You should go." When he tried to speak, she said, "*Please*. Just go."

He heard the door swing open and that was how it ended.

"I've got something new," he says, speaking softly against the door. "Comics—*3-D*. It's a big hit with the kids—comes with these paper glasses. Makes the pictures pop right off the page." He hears her padding about inside.

He'd given up trying to figure her out. Maybe her face was a train wreck. Or maybe she was a knockout or just plain, but married. It didn't matter. He would fill in the blanks, imagine her any way he wanted. He was, after all, a master at filling in the blanks.

"Look," he says. "I don't know what's going on. And I don't need to. I'll keep my hands to myself. . . okay?"

He waits a long time and then the door clicks open. He takes in every one of her fragrances—hears her reach in the bag for a comic, removing its wrapping.

"They're Japanese," he explains. "But who cares, right? It's the pictures that count."

"Wow," she says, flipping through the pages. He stands there with his arms at his sides. After a moment he feels the comic book slip past his hand back into the bag.

"*Wow*," she says again and he knows she is still wearing the glasses. He tries to remember what it was like to look through them as a kid—the tinted cellophane oddly coloring the world. He's certain she will keep them on.

"Come in," she says. "You know where the couch is."

How Joey Z. Saved Us All

Home Made

It was Joey taught us how to make a zip gun: car antenna for a barrel, a piece of two-by-four—the frame. Some friction tape to hold it all together. Rubber bands around a pointy nail to detonate the round—(a .22), and *Bam!*

It either put a hole in someone or blew up in your face. "50/50," Joey said. "The odds. Not bad."

Snap, Crackle and Pop

In a yard between the tenements, Joey built a fire—held out fat bullets stolen from his dad. Had us stand in a circle around the flames as he tossed them in. When the first round ricocheted against a wall, we scattered quick as sparrows, turned only from a distance as one by one the bullets popped and zinged—saw Joey, eyes shut, saying, "Shit! Holy shit!" His feet rooted where we left them.

How Joey Saved Us

On a rooftop, six stories higher than the street, than our stickball, our marbles and our ease, Joey called us "pussies" and "queers" 'cause no one volunteered to be the first to jump from roof to roof. Struck dumb among the pigeons on the sun-soft tar, we shrank beneath his disappointed gaze, as he stepped back, then back again and took a running leap. Landed on the other side. Just. A crunch against the sliding gravel edge. The sudden stop angling him back. His arms windmilling hard to make up for it, but not enough to fight the pull. The only sound, the word: *"Damn!"* coming from his upside-down face—his arms still spinning, then the faraway, almost too soft thud of him landing.

My mother's words coming back to me: *"You need to stop hanging out with that kid!"*

So I did.

Saw Blade

I talk Nina into it; Ed goes along. Neither can figure why I'm still pining over Gloria.

The three of us have a musical saw band. Pass the hat most times. Carry around these small collapsible garden seats. Sit under Gloria's window, the saws between our knees, bending and bowing Gloria's favorite: *Head Like a Hole*.

Her window's open and I'm hoping she'll find the sorrowful tones, the sweet sentiment, irresistible. But I'm beginning to think she's not home, till it starts raining some of my paperbacks. Troopers that we are, we keep playing. One by one they're flying out. And then this shirtless guy with a plethora of angry animal tattoos sticks his head out, says, "Get lost you crazy fucks!" as a hand snakes around his waist and eases him back in. The fingernails painted *Cayenne Pepper Red*. Gloria's favorite go-to shade.

We stop and Nina picks up one of the books, coos: "*Baudelaire*. Can I have it?"

I nod and we pack up. *Los Guanacos* is a couple of streets down and if the mariachis aren't there, we've got a spot.

Nina looks at me as we head off, Baudelaire in a reverential clutch. "Nothing like a saw," she says. "To cut through all the bullshit."

Mime with a Gun

A mime breaks into our house. He has a gun. We are watching TV in bed and my wife screams, pulls the blankets up to her chin. He turns up the set, puts a finger to his lips. We stare in silence. He's wearing a Spandex outfit and his face is painted geisha-white with a red star on either cheek.

He approaches us as if pushed back in a wind storm, struggling to advance. He does it so well, I nearly get the impression his hair is blown back. If we weren't so terrified, we might applaud. He does the trapped-in-the-box routine and drops his gun to the rug. When I move to the edge of the bed, he picks it back up quickly, wags a finger at me.

I shrug, afraid to speak—suddenly in a land where visuals trump all sound. He slips the gun into his armpit and points to his ringed finger, then runs his hands down from either side of his neck, coming together V-shaped.

"Necklace?" my wife says, suddenly playing charades with him. He nods.

"You want to steal our jewelry?" I add. He nods again and smiles. I sit up and put my hands over my head and cringe as if the ceiling were falling down upon me. I rub my head, creating the shape of a bump rising up. I scrunch up my face in pain. He watches, making a sad puppy dog expression. I count out imaginary dollar bills onto the covers. Then do a *poof!*-pantomime with my hands, fanning them and letting them fly up as if exploding into nothingness. I run my fingers down my cheeks—a flood of tears.

He puts his hands to his head in an "Oh-my-God" gesture and his face does a rubbery, crestfallen collapse into empathy. He takes the gun from his armpit and puts it into a Spandex pocket, where you can see every detail, turns and walks toward the door in slow motion. He's really good. He does an electric shock bit when he touches the doorknob, then waves over his shoulder as he exits. I hear a window slam shut in the kitchen downstairs and a car speed off.

I get up and hurry to the closet, grab my baseball bat and put it by the bed. You never know when a wayward juggler or a clown gone bad might be casing the neighborhood.

Ash and a Thousand Cranes

My best friend Ash has ordered this "Muscle Man" costume online and these fake prison tattoos. The muscle man rig has two halves that fasten with Velcro. It's made of plastic and he puts it on under his clothes when he goes out. He no longer wears his glasses and moves around like a robot.

It's a pretty rough neighborhood they've just moved to since his pop's been out of work. Nobody's really seen the beanpole Ash actually is.

"Whataya think?" he asks, his head looking way too small for the rest of him.

"Like one nasty hombre," I say. He beams.

"Damn it, Clyde!" his mother yells from the next room and Ash's younger brother runs in and ducks behind the couch. He begins biting the heads off several cranes. Their mom is making a thousand origami cranes to try and cure their dad's cancer, and stringing them together is supposed to grant you one enormous wish. Ash's mom caught wind of it at one of her support groups and now there's a box filled and hundreds draped everywhere.

Clyde keeps snatching them off the table and biting their heads off. He saw an old Tyrone Power movie where the actor becomes a sideshow geek at the end and decided that's what he wanted to be when he grew up. So now he's practicing.

"Bet you could stop a blade with that thing," I say and Ash bangs on a six pack bundle of hard plastic abs with his knuckles, says, "*Ouch.*"

We see Clyde poke his head out, eyeballing the cat. The cat spots him and scurries through the flap in the door out back.

"Hold this," Ash says. I take his mother's make-up mirror and hold it up so he can put a crudely inked teardrop tattoo on his cheek and a dagger coming up from his collar.

"How's your pop doing?" I ask. He doesn't say anything, just shrugs.

"I need cigarettes," his mom calls out. "Go to the corner store and get me some smokes." She nearly knocks over a bottle of gin reaching for her purse, which she has to dig out from under a pile of paper birds.

"Sure," Ash says, his little head all smiles. He looks ready.

Crescendos

They kept the Christmas decorations up year round. Chili pepper lights instead of icicles around the windows and a single reindeer and sled on the rooftop.

She played cymbals in an orchestra, and he felt it appropriate because of her propensity for crescendos, even with the smallest moments.

He was unemployed. An artist who tried to sell his paintings online. His *Fire* series. Each canvas ablaze with reds and yellows, screaming with light. There was never any smoke. The walls were covered with them.

Once, she'd told him, it was like living in Hell. But the connection eluded him. Looking up from his easel, he told her to get over herself.

Mr. Nasty

I let her in through the garage. She was older than I'd imagined and prettier. As she hurried past, her backpack brushed my chest.

"Sorry I'm late," she said. "You got somewhere I can change?"

I took her to a small bathroom in the back I never got around to finishing. Above us, the migrating herd of five-year-old girls thundered through the house. And the slow meandering patter of their parents could be heard, shuffling back and forth from the buffet table, and my wife of course, whizzing about with her egg-timer brain in a tizzy—her mother close behind, I was certain, soaking up every detail with her camcorder.

"Here, help me with this," she said, spinning around and tapping the back of her dress with a long lacquered nail. As I drew closer, I took in the contrasting scents of perfume and perspiration. I found them equally appealing. Her make-up was heavy for the role, her hair up in a tight bun.

"You're not bashful, are you?"

"You mean like the dwarf?" She laughed.

I put my beer bottle in my other hand and pulled down on the zipper. She wiggled her shoulders free and let the dress fall to her feet and stepped out of it. She was in her bra and panties—scooped up the dress and folded it. I turned and edged toward the door.

"Stay," she said, "while I get ready."

I tried to hide the fact that I was gawking, but did so every chance I got.

"What's the Birthday Girl's name?"

"Kelly," I said. But it wasn't my daughter I was thinking

about. It was her mother, tearing down the stairs, ticking audibly. Wondering where the hell *Snow White* was.

The backyard was filled with sunlight and the kids were getting antsy. There were games to be played, a cake to light, and presents to open. Everything had to be "just so," and there was always my mother-in-law's watchful eye, monitoring each beer hissed open—the two of them tag-teaming me with that *look*. The one that said, *Get it together you dumb shit.*

She pulled a princessy gown out of her pack and I gazed now, full on, at her rear—the frilly blue panties, what filled them.

"Looks like you work out," I heard myself say, wishing I hadn't.

"How would you know *that?*" She turned, her heavily painted eyebrows arched.

"I. . ."

"Only kidding." She smiled. "I'm a gym rat. Can't get enough. Looks like you do all right yourself." She glanced over at my free weights in a corner of the next room.

"There's about three inches of dust on them," I told her.

She squeezed my bicep. "I don't think so." She pulled the gown over her head. "Here, give me some of that." She reached for the bottle and took a swig; pulled a breath mint out of her pack and popped it.

I stared at the lipstick on the mouth of the bottle as she handed it back. It was a sight I hadn't seen in years. She followed my eyes and tore off a sheet of toilet paper. "Let me get that," she said.

I shook my head and put the bottle to my lips and drained most of it. She slipped into a glittery pair of red pumps and put the folded dress in the pack. Grabbed a shiny black wig from another compartment and put it on, squinted into the mirror, brushing down the bangs with her hand. "So," she said, looking at me in the mirror. "If you're not Bashful, which one are you?"

The migrating wildebeests rumbled down the hall and I heard what sounded like a bowling ball dropped. "You mean the Seven Dwarfs?"

"Or the eighth, if you like." Her face brightened.

Nasty, I thought. I'd be *Mr. Nasty*. "Let me think about it," I told her.

"Don't take *too* long," she said. "That little cottage in the woods is getting pretty crowded." She handed me a card over her shoulder without turning. "I don't only work with kids. I do private parties too." She gave me a look that wouldn't quit. I put the card in my pocket. It was not the cartoony one my wife had pressed against the fridge with a bunny magnet.

"I'd better go up the front way," she said. "A princess must always maintain her dignity." I imagined some of the other costumes she had in her collection. She was a shape-shifter, right now out of Disney. But I could still feel her inside—another character altogether.

"I'd be Mr. Na. . ." I began. But I couldn't get it out.

"What?"

"Forget it," I told her, thinking how 17 years of marriage can give you lockjaw sometimes. I pulled back the beer and emptied it, opened the garage door and listened to it rattle up. Then Snow White glided up the steps and rang the bell.

Sun-Ripe

He jumps off the back of the garbage truck into the snow. The plows precede him, scraping a narrow path. The cans are nearly buried. He digs them out.

He glimpsed a head once, a woman's head ripped out of a trash bag and crushed into the compactor; a blue eye staring up at him. He found out later it belonged to a mannequin. The things you put up with sometimes.

When he told Emma, she laughed. He views mannequins differently now, their blank stares at the mall. This time it's a can filled with flip flops, many of them crusted with sand. In every color. Some neon bright with fat plumerias, green palms, glowing against the snow-dotted trash.

How many beaches? he thinks. And what brought them to this point, this place? There are two very different sizes. A break-up perhaps. Or maybe one beach too many. All those hot suns beating down on them.

He thinks of all the vacations he's promised Emma. Christ, they keep coming, scattering, brightening the rubble. Till the compactor has its final say. And there is only the snow coming down and his breath smoking out in front of him and the next can and the next—the usual stuff.

A Fork in the Neck

I was eating from a carton of Chinese takeout, with half a load on, when I heard someone come in through the open door in the back. I hid behind the wall and when I saw him turn toward the kitchen, I plunged my fork in his neck.

He stood there with his jaw swung open and his eyes bugged out looking at me—the fork moving up and down as he yelled, "What the fuck?" A trickle of blood darkened his collar.

"You idiot! You stabbed me!" He screeched.

Damn! I thought, as it came to me. He looked like my neighbor, Bill—sort of. *Damn, damn, damn.*

He reached for the fork and I shouted, "No!—don't touch that. It might really start bleeding if you pull it out."

"It hurts like a sonofabitch."

"You're Bill's brother."

"No shit," he said. "My nephew knocked his ball over your fence."

"Christ. I'm sorry. I thought. . ."

"Screw what you thought. Call 911!"

"I'll drive you," I told him. "It'll be quicker."

As I tore through traffic, I saw him looking in the visor mirror, holding the end of the fork and grumbling to himself. I wondered if there was Kung Pao Chicken coursing through an artery—hoping there wasn't one of those little red pepper chips I loved so much, on the end of the fork.

At the E.R. they rushed him through, and I tagged along, sheepishly. The attending physician swooped in with a gaggle of residents in tow, but it turned out it didn't hit anything vital, mostly muscle and he didn't even need a stitch. But they gave him a shot, and gave me "a look" when they heard the story. And I thought for a minute they might call the law on me. But he insisted it was an accident and they let it drop.

On the way back we talked—mainly me saying what a dumb shit I was for not giving him a chance to explain before letting him have it. I could tell he'd feel a lot better if he could just toss me out the window on the freeway. He was a pretty big guy and I remember Bill mentioning his younger brother—the football star in high school that got all the babes and even played a bit in college.

I shook his hand when we got out of the car, and I felt my fingers crunch. A small payback perhaps for the neck jewelry I contributed so freely. Bill and his wife and three kids came out and it all was explained, everyone staring at the large bandage covering one side of his neck—at the little red dots at the center of it. Then, the group as one, turned toward me, glowering.

I went back in and sat in the kitchen, wondering if I should call Tina at her sister's, where she always went after one of our big blow-outs. Decided she considered me a gigantic asshole as it was, and this would move me to a *black hole in space* status I'd be better off without. I'd lost my appetite by then, thinking of that look on Bill's brother's face when I asked the doctor for the fork back. It was a favorite from a set Tina and I got as a wedding present. I put it in the sink and ran some hot water over it. I pulled a beer from a six pack and figured I'd be doing some serious damage to the other five.

Later that night, I went out in the yard with a flashlight and found the ball under some Sweet Williams my wife was always fussing over, worse-for-wear since she'd been gone. It was quiet. It was very late. I tossed the ball over the fence and listened for its soft thump as it landed.

Fun House

She'd gotten the fun house mirrors at an auction and had them put up in the spare bedroom. He found them strange, even a little disturbing, and thought the buy extravagant with the kids away at college and the big tuition bucks spilling out. But she'd insisted on a "well deserved splurge" after all that *straight and narrow*. A side of her, new to him.

So he went along. Even following her one night, with a bottle of Marques de Riscal, into that room with the lights dimmed and candles she placed on both dressers, adding to the mix. In bed, she began taking off her clothes, then his. "No way," he said, draining the last of the wine, gazing into one of the mirrors overhead, at their stretched-out, undulating forms; fleshy waves of them in the sheets.

He started to sit up, but she pulled him back. "This is weird, Connie," he said.

She reached out a zigzaggy hand and ran it down his zigzaggy middle. Looking left, she was squat and condensed, her cheeks bulged as if she had two apples stuffed in her mouth—her breasts large, wobbly globes. She guided his hand to them.

In another, the two of them were amoeboid, transforming silvery strangers. "You've got to be kidding me," he said. She smiled. And at a glance it was an astonishingly wide curl, liquid as mercury. He continued shifting his vision.

"My God!" he said.

"What?"

"The size of that thing."

She leaned over and whispered something. A name, he thought—not his own. Perhaps an endearment. She shook out her hair—jagged bolts against his chest. He closed his eyes, and when he opened them, she was wriggly and rosy. A stick figure, a block, a fleshy smear—strange and elegant. He heard some low, guttural sounds—his own.

She bit his shoulder and he pulled her close. His eyes banged against each corner of their sockets. The room was cluttered. It was ablaze with candlelight—squat fiery balls, elongated licks of light, and all their odd and flagrant infidelities in every piece of glass.

Uncategorized Omen

A sparrow flew out of the carcass of our Thanksgiving turkey one year, and flapped about, batting into everything. My mother screamed. And Grandmother crossed herself and said it was a *sign*.

"What sign?" my mother snapped, wide-eyed, nearly hysterical. Grandmother shrugged.

"Probably came in the window to get some stuffing," my father explained.

"What sign?" Mother insisted.

"I don't know that one," Grandmother told her.

The bird was getting dangerously close to the ceiling fan as it circled.

"Quick, turn it off!" my mother shouted. We opened all the windows and the front and back doors and it finally flew out. We watched it sail through the yards till it was a dot, then nothing at all. Mother sat down in the kitchen and lit up—glared at the skeleton on the table.

The game was clicked off in the living room and everyone sat back down at the table. My father poured the wine.

"Without really knowing—good/bad—I'd say 50/50," Grandmother announced. "Probably even better odds 'cause it didn't hit the fan."

Mother sighed out a stream of smoke. "I'll take it," she said finally, and we held up our glasses and clicked them, even us kids with our cream sodas. Then we all took a sip to seal the deal.

Goin' Country

"Nam, alcohol, shitty jobs, break-ups. . . Christ!" he says. "You lucky bastard. Hey, tell me about Rita. How she screwed you over. *Screwed. . ."* He muses for a moment, holding a pencil over a small pad like a nosy detective. "Screw-driving woman. . . Screwed by her screwin' around. . . Nah."

He's a friend of a friend from work. A pharmacist— wants to give up his cushy life to be a country singer/song writer, but lacks an ass-whoopin' life to draw from. He's picking my brain for scabs still red around the edges.

"She's gone," I say. "It's that simple." I hold up the bottle. "Let me introduce you to an old friend," I tell him, try not to screw up my face as the tequila goes down.

He thinks for a minute, writes. *"That bottle's now a best friend of mine,"* he sings in an off-key, scratchy voice. "Humm. . . Hey, that a picture of her—*the perp?"*

He points, knocking over a framed photo of me and my ex-wife. "Fuck off fella!" I say, standing now, ready to chuck him out like a sack of shit.

"That's good," he says. "The alliteration, I mean. But don't think I can use it—the cussin' and all." He scoots closer. "But what else you got?"

Grenades

She gazed at his socks in the drawer left open. That first month. They were in a row meticulously rounded and tucked into themselves. "They look like avocados from a Thiebaud painting," she said. "So elegant. So precise." He stepped out of the bathroom, still damp from the shower, with a toothbrush tilting sideways in his mouth, a bit of foam on his chin. He pushed the drawer shut. *"Avocados,"* he said, mumbling through the toothpaste and plastic, folding a tissue neatly and slowly into quarters, wiping away the foam.

One of These Is Not a Family Legend (Multiple Choice)

(A)

The doorbell rings. When I open it, my wife rips past on the back of a Harley. I put my hands over my ears. It barely helps.

"I forgot my lipstick," she says, as the Hell's Angel stops outside a small bathroom off the hall. She leaps from the bike and goes in. He's revving the engine while he waits. "Come on doll," he says.

When she gets back, she straddles the bike and leans forward, painting her lips in the side view mirror—a color (something in the pomegranate family) I've never seen. "Luscious," he says, reaching behind and patting her thigh, then slowly turns the bike around and roars past me down the steps and into the street.

(B)

There's a knock at the door. My ex is on the stoop hugging a framed photo of us. A stringy flop of hair shadows her face. "I can't sleep," she says, "I've missed you so. I've made a horrible mistake. No one else can compare. They're all sniveling wimps compared to you. *God!* What was I thinking?"

"You look chilled," I tell her.

"You know how to fix that. You were always good at fixing that." She reaches out a shaky hand, and that charm bracelet I got her in Mexico jingles a bit.

"I'm sorry, Jule," I say. "But there's. . ."

Just then Alicia (Cassandra is showering upstairs) comes clicking down the hall in those spiked heels and little else. "Who is it, Babe?" she asks as I shut the door, and all the street sounds vanish.

(C)

It's the postman. A package from Amazon. I'd gotten my six-year-old, *The Big Book of Butterflies*. But she said, "When you don't look at the wings, they're just a bunch of creepy bugs." I ask how her mom is doing. She says, "Fine."

She visits now only on the weekends. I fashion tents made of sheets held together by clothespins (the alligator kind), draped over chairs, spread wide apart. There is a sleeping bag inside, a 13" TV, and a plethora of naked Barbies all speaking in different pitches of her voice.

I take the box and thank him. It contains a book of "snowflakes" this time. Each showcased on a slick page. Each a miraculously individual design.

Later, I will hear her Barbies cooing over it as I clip on a few more pins. When her head pokes out, finally, she tells me, "It's really nice, Dad. But maybe we should keep it in the freezer." I do.

Twisted

The kids loved him. He kept telling her so. It's where he fit in best. Clammed up around her friends, the dog suddenly more interesting, the view, the lint he hunted up from the couch.

He kept making these balloon animals she never recognized. "Platypus," he'd tell her. But she'd see only a pile of sausages. All that was missing was the plate.

Christmas, he did a balloon nativity scene and she listened to that squeaky rubber-rub sound as he twisted them into shape, the Wise Men appearing as taut red snakes twisted into themselves she kept hoping would pop.

Uncle L

My Uncle L is in the rec lounge of the *Leafy Cottage* rest home—a narrow room with parrot-green walls and a TV turned up nearly to distortion.

He's slumped in his wheelchair with Mr. Mumps on his lap. Mr. Mumps does all the talking these days, his high-pitched voice still making cracks—my Uncle L behind him moving his lips.

Since his stroke, Uncle L talks out of one corner of a droopy mouth that looks as if it were made of wax that had melted, working the controls in Mr. Mumps' back, making his eyes move, his head swing from side to side, his jaw flap. My uncle has shrunk down even further in his PJs since I've seen him last. I sit in a small plastic chair, thinking how to tell him my dad won't be visiting anymore. That he's in the ground now with all their other siblings. That Uncle L's the only one left.

My dad used to come, two, three times a week, and they'd sit together. My father always got a kick out of whatever shred of a joke Mr. Mumps came up with. He visited nearly to the end.

"Hi Uncle L," I say. "I got you some sweets." I put the big bag of M&Ms on his lap and Mr. Mumps leans forward to look at it. "Did you hear the one about the nun and the talking cucumber?" Mr. Mumps asks in that squeaky voice. "No," I say, moving my chair closer. Behind me, from the TV, I hear Lucy and Ethel cooking up another hair-brained scheme. "Me neither," the dummy says, his eyebrows bouncing up and down.

"I wanted to talk to you, Uncle L," I say.

"Who are you?" Mr. Mumps asks, his voice a little raspy.

"I'm your nephew, Al—your brother Peter's kid."

"You got vodka?" it asks, and I find myself talking to the dummy just like I did growing up. Even in his diminished state, he can still bring the doll to life.

In the old days he played major clubs with his dummies. Even toured Vietnam, with a hippy doll he had, to entertain the troops. And before that was booked to do Sullivan, but was bumped, as he liked saying, "By those four mop-heads from England." Mr. Mumps was always his favorite.

"They won't let you have that here," I say, and Mr. Mumps gives me the raspberry.

I switch from looking at the doll's puffy red cheeks into my uncle's eyes, blank as buttons. "Your brother Peter won't be able to make it here anymore."

"Who?" The doll's head swings back and forth.

"But I'll try and come as often as I can." I point to the bag in his lap. "You want some M&Ms?"

"Who are you?"

"Al," I tell him, pulling his afghan up. "Your nephew, Al."

When I was six he made me a hand puppet using an old sock and my mother's lipstick to paint a face. I kept it for years, filling our old dog Sudsy's ears with rambling monologues till the cotton was worn thin. "You look good," I say.

"One more and I'll have enough for a golf course," Mr. Mumps says.

On the TV, Lucy's face collapses as Ricky stands over her grimacing, his hands on his hips. The room fills with raucous canned laughter.

"Anyway, like I was saying—your brother Peter won't be able. . ."

An elderly woman enters then with an armload of magazines. When she bends to place them on the coffee table, Uncle L issues a loud fart-sound out of the corner of his mouth and she straightens.

"Laurence. . ." she chides, playfully. He always hated the name Laurence. It was his father's and they never got along.

"Hear the one about the tax collector and the bowl of Jell-O?" Mr. Mumps blares, his eyes jetting in her direction.

"Would you like some Jell-O, Laurence?" she says. "Is that what you're trying to say?"

"Vodka," the dummy insists.

"What a kidder," she says, waving a mock parental finger at Mr. Mumps on her way out.

I turn back and Mr. Mumps' head swings around at the same time. "But don't worry," I say. "I'll try and come as. . ."

"Man walks into a bar with an octopus on his head," Mr. Mumps rasps now in my uncle's voice. Both are staring at the TV.

I get up and move his wheelchair over by the couch, in front of the set and sit beside him, take the bag of M&Ms from his lap. I open it and pick out the red ones, which were always Uncle L and my favorites. Mr. Mumps rests limply against his chest as my uncle looks down at the bright, sweet beads accumulating in his palm.

It's an episode of *I Love Lucy* I vaguely recognize, but can't recall how it ends. I lean back and we watch it.

The Saint of Redirection

I pray to the patron Saint of Redirection, who shows up juggling sardines and a large red apple he takes a bite out of every revolution or so.

"This life," I say. "The sheer weight of it. . ."

"Is that you?" he asks, letting the silvery circle collapse at his feet—slipping the apple in his pocket. He's pointing to an old photo. "No, that's my older brother, when we were kids. I'm the one. . ." I turn and see he's now rowing across the living room in a small boat. "Calm seas," he announces, skirting the TV. "I think it's going to be a magnificent voyage."

"I'm worried," I tell him. "This crazy world. It's so lopsided with evil ballooning out—I sometimes feel it'll slip right off its axis and hurl. . ."

"Nice drapes" he says, crawling up them like a cat. I look for tears, but there aren't any.

"And what's all this about an afterlife? Holy crap—who could ever know. . ."

"What's for lunch?" he asks.

"Humm. . . I hadn't thought about it. Chinese, I suppose."

He tosses a TV guide over with a startling cover, and I catch it. He turns for the door. "Oops," he says, as the enormous sombrero he's suddenly wearing gets wedged between the frame. "Could you give me a little shove?"

"Hey, thanks," I say as I push, and he pops out, audibly—heads off down the street on a wobbly tricycle.

I call *Yet Wah's*—order the Tangerine Beef. Get a cold one from the fridge and begin leafing through the guide. There'll be time enough later to clean up the fish.

Bite-sized

He climbs skyscrapers to unwind. Sees the irony in this. But after Trudy died, he found it most stressful just sitting around slowly drinking the minutes.

His hands have always been strong and the crowds below mean nothing to him; the cops waiting with cuffs, the clicking cameras. You block it out. Pace yourself. Everything depends on it. There is only the next crease in the wall. There are no vistas before you, only the startling ones at your back.

When his heart gets going like a hummingbird's, he pauses, remembers Trudy in that dress with the little mirrors sewn into it, the one that he got her in Mexico. How the world reflected, bite-sized.

A fireman above him calls, stretches a hand from a window, wants to drag him in and he veers to the side. There's still plenty of climb left. Figures, there is one of two ways this can go—and the fewer interruptions, the better.

Grandly Awesome

She decided she would leave him, but for now they lay naked and she wrote on his back with her finger. "Guess," she said. "G-r-a-n. . . *grandly.*" Then, "A-w-e-s-o. . . *Awesome*—grandly awesome. That it?" "That's you," she said, and he smiled, drew closer. She'd written: "Goodbye asshole"—plain and simple. Never *could* read me, she thought.

The Limits of Art
(A Fable)

Looking in the mirror, he sees a colossal flare of peacock feathers fan out behind him. *"Wow!"* He races to the *Bottoms Up Club* down the street, his folded plumes dragging behind him. If he can't score now, he thinks—he might as well hang it up.

It's packed inside with lots of women. He goes to the jukebox, slips in a coin and lets 'er rip—a feathery splendor slowly spreading nearly to the ceiling. The music comes on, and he does this little dance incorporating a quiver to the plume tips, which is apparently irresistible because five beauties, who wouldn't give him a hint of a tumble, minutes prior, surround him cooing like schoolgirls—their painted lips seductively parted.

Left, right—quiver, quiver—left, right. . . He's in the zone, when suddenly a fight breaks out. Two guys across from them, playing rough. One pulls back his hoodie, revealing a large pair of ram's horns; the other, the same. His fickle bevy scatters, reassembles for a closer look. Each man now on either end of the room, head down, poised to rocket.

He needs a drink, shuffles off, his long train trailing in the sawdust.

"What's your poison?" the barkeep says, above some puffy squeals—above the clash, the thunder.

Stick

It's a little past three in the afternoon when I find my grandmother on fire in the kitchen. It's just a small section of her sleeve and I pat it out, take the matches from her she used trying to light our electric burner.

At dinner she quietly forks up mashed potatoes my mother is prompting her to eat, the gravy pooled in the crater-like structure Mom's made of them, just like her mother fashioned for her as a kid.

Mind-weary is as close as my mother gets to explaining what is happening to Nana. And I say, "Oh." Picture her brain panting like a dog with its tongue hanging out after chasing a stick in the heat like our old dog Freckles, and nothing more is said of it.

Years later, Billy's dad drops dead in the shower and his mom is forced to work at the *Blue Bell Diner*. We take LSD at his house and are playing his dad's old Sinatra records at the wrong speed when Billy says he hears the devil speaking to him with an Italian accent.

"Listen—*there!*" he says.

But I'm too mind-weary at the moment to hear it, busy sniffing the wallpaper roses and hiding all the matches and wondering how a man's heart can explode like a bottle under a truck tire. Just like that. And thinking about Freckles, how all she needed was a stick—back and forth, back and forth—that little pink tongue hanging out and so happy afterwards just to lie down in the shade.

Pretzel Girl

She threw a head of red cabbage at me. If it were a bowling ball, it might have taken me out. Boy, did she have a temper. I was dating the Pretzel Girl from the circus. You can use your imagination as to what it was like in bed.

It was all innocent enough. I'd reached for this tomato on the pile. The reddest I'd ever seen, at the same time this attractive young lady did. We laughed as our hands collided and she told me I could have it. I smiled and told her she could. We went back and forth a bit more and she blushed, nearly as red. But in the end, she gave it a good feel and slipped it into her bag. When she moved over to the cucumber section, that's when the cabbage flew.

Waiting in the checkout line, my girlfriend stooped down and tied her shoe. She could have bent over backwards and done it that way. No kidding, it's like she has no bones. When she took a carton of milk from the cart, I flinched. I grabbed up a tabloid and began paging through it. The remains of a small being were found in the woods in Alabama, believed to be that of an extraterrestrial. The remnants of a large boat were discovered atop a mountain that scientists maintain was Noah's. There was no mention of the Pretzel Girl killing her new boyfriend with a flung food item. I wanted to keep it that way.

I placed several of her favorite candy bars on the conveyer belt and gave her my best *look-honey-bunny* grin. If she were barefooted, she could easily have reached a leg over her shoulder and picked them up with her toes. And believe me when I tell you—there's a lot to be said for a thing like that.

Strings

The chill was still in Ray's old bones as he watched the four bottles of gin, his stiff little soldiers, advance on the conveyer belt toward the cashier. He added a tabloid paper in their wake; took his wallet out and pointed it at the fuzzy flying saucer photo on the cover.

"I wish they'd abduct *me*," he said. "I keep waiting. Maybe they can do something about this arthritis."

The cashier smiled. Her make-up was caked over a few small patches of acne. She looked fresh out of high school. He gazed at her name tag. It said *Summer*. She shifted her weight uneasily, thinking he was staring at her breasts.

"Nice name to have this time of year," he said.

"Yeah," she said, "thanks."

The line behind him was starting to grow and she began double bagging. The bottles tapped together—a familiar music.

"I used to have this crush on a puppet once," he said. And when he reached down into his wallet she glanced over at the woman fidgeting behind him and rolled her eyes.

"Before your time. She was named after all *four* seasons. Something like Princess Winter-Spring-Summer-Fall. Or, Summer-Spring-Winter-Fall. I forget which. A real cutie. I mean for a puppet. But when you're a kid, they seem so real—you know?"

The girl nodded.

"Howdy Doody Show," he said. "You hear of it? Way back with the dinosaurs."

She swung the price indicator facing him. "I'm not sure," she said. "Maybe."

He handed her a bill. She placed the change on the

counter. His fingers were curled into themselves and he struggled to lift them.

"Here. . ." she said, reaching out. But he'd already swept the coins in his other hand and into his pocket.

"They had great shows for kids back then."

She smiled, ringing up the next customer. "Well, you have a nice day," she said, suddenly summery.

He noticed the small green gem imbedded in one side of her nose. He wondered if it was real or just a piece of glass.

In the parking lot he looked up at the sky. There's snow in those clouds, but no spacemen, he thought. Too bad. There was a thing or two about a thing or two he'd like to ask.

He put the bags on the seat next to him. The bottles tapped together with a glassy music. It was his lucky day. The car started right up.

Slugs

My wife yells from the kitchen, and I know that they are back. They come only at night, squeeze under the door like paste to get to the cat's food—small dry stars that stick to an end, a non-face, an impossible-to-imagine mouth.

Two floors up they crawl from the garden—a slow-motion peristalsis that scoffs at wings. How long must it take? we muse. Is this their mountain temple? Their holy trough? Or merely an all-night diner worth the wait?

For months now I've been throwing them back. They land with a gentle sound, only to begin again. Lately, I've been flushing them down the toilet in a swirl of justice. Tonight I refuse. My wife holds one wrapped in a paper towel like a sloppy coat. Recently they have entered her dreams. She holds it out, her face screwed tight, as though it might, through some miracle of motion, suddenly lunge. If there is a struggle, it is too slow to perceive—a cry unheard.

"Come on, take it," she pleads, her reverence for nature, tainted by abhorrence. "No," I say. "Blood must change hands. It's only fair."

Her body bends under this burden of reason. I hear a muted plop—picture its paper shroud: a colorful print of grapefruits and oranges—descent into the maelstrom, still clutching its prize.

When she returns she is pale, and a new paste has squeezed to the altar. "Never again," she hisses. "They can have the damn cat's food!"

Cancer Pot

They met at their mother's house to decide which of her possessions to divide and what to toss. In a small drawer they found the medical marijuana. Her sister called it "cancer pot," which made the tight fragrant buds a little creepy.

They took it out to the garden and rolled a fat one. Smiled, as they recalled how their mother would crack open the door to their bedroom, when they were teens, giggling through thick clouds on the edge of the bed. How only that hand entered, choking them with half a can of air freshener whenever her *men friends* came calling.

Irony was never mentioned.

A dog in the next yard, a little yapper, was doing its thing. Letting the world know it was there. In the garden, crawling about or waiting in lacy strings, there was much that didn't.

Three quarters of the way down, the yapper started getting to them. A seed popped and they jumped. There was little left of the begonias against the fence.

Hubba-Hubba

She came into the kitchen wearing the rabbit ears, tilted on top of her rollers. The Playboy Bunny ears she wore when she was a blond at the Club serving cocktails and he was grabbing her ass whenever he could.

He was retired now, but bartended a few days a week at *Suds & Buds*, and she was a professional bingo caller, adding to the till.

"B-34," she called out sharply, and he looked up from his paper. "34-B is more like it," he said. It was their little joke. She was many times that now.

"Found it in a box downstairs." He noticed one of the ears had been eaten by something—a moth or a mouse. It was slightly mildewed. She posed for him in her robe, swinging it open and then shut quickly, as if the blur of a glimpse might shave away the years. "Hubba-hubba," he said and took a sip of coffee and lit a cigarette. "You still got it, Kiddo."

She sat down and the thing slid a little more to one side. He removed a section of news and handed it to her, then folded what was left neatly and resumed reading it.

First Date

"I'm looking for shatter-proof scenarios this time," she said, putting on her Teflon vest and freshening her lipstick. "You know, the kinds that don't blow up in your face. Or if they do, it's only confetti—a light sprinkling you can just shake out of your hair. Know what I mean? Where the knives are rubber and falling rocks are paper mache, like in those old "B" movies. Ones you can kick out of your way even if you were bare-footed. You get it, right?"

"Sure," I said, slipping on my shark-proof mail-lined gloves and ordering the lobster. "At our age, who wouldn't?"

"I like you," she said. "I think. I mean I'm pretty sure. And I'm glad you invited me." She leaned closer, knocking over her untouched drink. We both watched it spread into the table cloth. "I'm told, not only the food, but the food tasters here are excellent. *The ones that have made it,*" she whispered.

"Second to none," I told her.

More of the Same

Evie was painting her toenails when Steve said, "Hell, I could use a few more of you. Have a ménage `a. . . How do you say *eight* in French?"

They were watching a program on cloning and he was already ruminating on some of its appealing applications. "They," he said, "could start at the top and bottom of yours truly and work their way to the middle".

She paused, the polish brush suspended just over her "Pretty in Pink" Tootsie toe dividers. "You tryin' to tell me something, Steve?"

"They'd all be *you*, hon," he reassured. "That's the best part."

"Well, I could use a few more of *you* too," she said, thinking maybe a few of those "fix-it" projects he kept promising might actually get done.

"You mean it?" he said.

"Sure."

He imagined what it would be like, (a bunch of Steves) ravaging her all at once. And they'd all be him doing it. He could hardly wait for her nails to dry.

Steve stretched out on the couch. Hell, he thought, he might even have his harem get boob jobs in different sizes. And they could all wear wigs. He didn't care what color—blue, purple. . . Variety was what he was after. He imagined the all-nighters.

"So, you think it'd be hot having a bunch of me around?" Steve said, edging closer. "You really meant that?"

"Uh-huh," she said, spotting a cuticle that needed clipping.

He took a magazine from the coffee table and began fanning her feet, nearly clubbing her big toe.

"What are you doing?"

"Helping 'em dry."

"That's all right," she said, dipping the little brush back in the bottle. "I'm doing my fingernails now."

"Christ," he said and flung down the magazine. He grabbed the remote and began flipping through the channels.

Evie watched him for a long moment, then threw up her hands. *"What?"*

The Ghost Gets a Visit

"I was *The Ghost*," he said to the woman sitting next to him on the edge of the bed. There was a small TV playing on a chair across from them. A soap opera. A young actress weeping and some guy in a suit sweet-talking her into or out of something—she couldn't tell which.

"That was my moniker," he said, pointing to a shrine-like clutter of framed photos of him thirty years younger. One, with another wrestler he held over his head easily as a bag of laundry.

"Wow," she said. "Great outfit."

"It was mostly a sheet. A fancy one with cut-outs. A rhinestone collar. Silk, though. The sheet was real silk. I was always slipping out of holds. Disappearing sort of. That's why they called me *The Ghost*."

"Quite a Hall of Fame," she said.

"I was something once," he said.

Jerry, the desk clerk, had told her he wouldn't quibble over the price. *The Ghost* could play it any way he wanted, she thought. Hey, yapping counted, if that's all it was.

She saw him glance down briefly at her breasts. "They're all mine," she said.

He patted his chest. "That makes two of us," he said, referring to the colossal avalanche that had occurred.

"Gravity's a bitch." She tapped her rear.

He smiled. There were a couple of teeth missing. "Wasn't always like that," he said. "Was a time I could rip a phone book in half, easy as shit."

"You mind if I light up?"

He shrugged.

She took a long puff and blew the smoke out of the corner of her mouth, away from him.

"You read that one yet?" She reached down picking a slim paperback from a stack of them by the side of the bed.

"Read 'em all," he said.

"Think you can rip this one in half?"

"You kidding? Here, give me that other one too." He lined up the two slender novels and worked his enormous hands around them, twisting back and forth. He bit his lip till a small tear in the pages widened. After a great effort, the books split apart.

"Wow!" she said, one eye squinted shut from the cigarette in her mouth, and clapped. She squeezed his bicep with what little of her hand she could wrap around it. "You still got it," she said.

"Small potatoes." He tossed the book pieces down. "I bet I could lift you over my head and hold you there with one hand."

She gazed at him for a moment without speaking.

"I'll hold you over the bed if you like."

She took a long drag, then let her cigarette drop into an empty beer can on the floor. "Okay, I guess. But you be careful. You be damn careful."

"No sweat," he said, having her lie flat on the bed with her arms at her sides. "Make your body stiff," he said. "Yeah, like that."

He put his hands under her, drew in a few deep breaths. She closed her eyes and felt the world drop away, and when she opened them again she was staring at the ceiling. She heard him grunt as he gingerly took one hand away. She turned her head and could see the veins in his neck bulged out—his face red and contorted.

"Don't move," he said, his voice tight. Almost imperceptibly, he turned her shakily to the left and then the right.

"Oh, Daddy," she said. *"Oh, Daddy."* And she thought she heard him groan, but it was muffled and indistinct. She tilted, bracing herself as his arm dipped. But he grabbed her quickly with both hands again and lowered her down slowly into the sheets.

She lay there quietly and watched him huffing and swaying like a giant that had just jumped off a carousel. Noticed a tattoo dagger twitch as he stood there. Then he sat in a chair by the wall and slowly took off his shoes. Then his pants. Got up and draped them over the TV.

The actress in the soap was in a different scene by a marina. Tearless now, she was letting somebody really have it. But the woman watching, as *The Ghost* approached, could no longer tell who.

Nose Job

I visit my brother at that place again with the TV going and everyone walking around like zombies. He's in a wheelchair doing wheelies. His legs are fine; he's just being ornery is all. He's good at it. He lights up when he sees me. Avoids the zombie bit by pretending to take his meds and spitting them out later. He's still the same pistol he was growing up. The older brother I looked up to before he whacked out.

When we get to the lounge, we begin talking at cross purposes again. It's what we do these days. Sometimes checking in with a nod now and then. Not much more.

"I saw that poltergeist again," he says, sitting next to me on the couch. "The one with red panties. She's mostly light, a kind of yellow light. But the panties are red."

"I think Karen's cheating on me," I tell him. "I can smell him on her. Subtle stuff, like a soap she never uses."

"They're frilly," he says, "and I can almost make out a bra. I think. But the light hurts my eyes if I look too long."

I've got this job, product testing different formulas. I do "taste and sniff" discernments for a big company. It's all about focusing and blocking every other sense out but the one you're working with.

"I think it's *Old Spice*," I say. "A faint hint of it—his deodorant. And his sunscreen once on her."

My brother gets up and sits back in the wheelchair, facing the TV. He thinks space creatures are trying to contact him through the set. At least that's what I think he said a couple of visits back.

"She denies it of course. But I've noticed she's taking a

lot more showers lately."

He looks at me, "Huh?" Then turns back.

"Voosh ikzt mekric," my brother says, wheeling closer to the TV.

"You'd think she'd be more careful," I say. "Knowing what I do and all." I look over and see a woman on the screen with great puckered lips putting her face up close to a product I've tested. She smiles and an exaggerated super nova glistens from her teeth.

"Yes, yes. . ." my brother says, his face against the smiling beauty—a blinding light behind him coming in from the window, but no red panties. "Yes, okay." He nods. "Fuckin' A!"

And I smile over at my brother, happy to know the creatures have finally learned the Queen's English. It's a start.

Dirty Eyeballs

After Korea, Billy's uncle, who stayed at Billy's house for a while, came back a little screwy. "Nerves" was the way they explained it. He'd take the centers out of slices of white bread and shape them into small, tight balls. The doctors said it might help.

All day he'd roll them, over and over between his thumb and fingertips like worry stones, till they all turned black—a beer in one hand, a doughy ball in the other—working it, working it. . .

Whenever we'd go to Billy's house, we'd see them everywhere, like dirty eyeballs staring up at us from sofas, countertops, sinks—a creepy pile of them in the ashtray on the coffee table in front of the TV.

The Cleaning Girl

It was great having the house to herself. That big, fancy house. She went into the cow's bedroom and sat down on the edge of the bed. It had a memory foam topper and she pressed her hand into it, was endlessly amused watching the imprint vanish. Now that the bed was stripped, she was looking forward to pressing her whole body into it.

The cow's husband was on the dresser beside her, and there were those tricky eyes of his that were always on her when the cow wasn't looking. When he'd smile and she'd smile back.

She got up and went through the top drawer where the jewelry was kept—all that glitter wasted. What, after all, did a cow need with jewelry? She put the necklaces on first, the pearls, the gold chains, the teardrop diamonds. Then the rings, which kept slipping off. So she held her hands up as though she were drying her nails, finally deciding to put them on her thumbs.

She took one of the special bras from a drawer, red and lacy—new looking like it had never been worn, and put it on over her small breasts. She took several of the husband's socks and stuffed each cup. It felt good having something of his against her. She looked in the mirror, shifted her weight from one foot to the other, tilted her head, smiled coyly. He'd like that, she thought. She twisted out some lipstick, *Berry Burst*, and painted her lips, breeching the edges and getting some on her teeth.

She brushed her long hair down over one eye and peeked out through it; the room appealingly striated. She was reaching for some bracelets when the doorbell rang. She froze for a moment as though the stillness might make her invisible. Then she pictured the cow at the door with an armload of packages. She scrambled in a panic. It rang again. She broke for the kitchen and grabbed her coat, buttoned it up tight. *The rings!* She slid them off and into her pockets.

Not only would she be fired, she'd probably be arrested. Even though she hadn't intended to steal anything. But what would that matter. The cow would see to it that it wouldn't matter. She'd say she had a chill when she was questioned about the coat. She was sick and needed to go home. She'd put the jewelry back when she could. She hurried to the door and opened it.

Two smartly dressed women with good posture stood there grinning, one much older than the other. *JOHOS!*

"Can we…" the older one began, holding out a pamphlet with a glowing Christ on the cover seeming to levitate.

"Shit," she said. "Just go!" She swung the door shut and bolted to the bedroom, slipping off the necklaces as she did. She put everything back and sat on the edge of the bed with the coat on her lap, panting. Decided she'd keep the lipstick on, right where it belonged. The cow and the gawker looked at her from a gilded frame. She gave them both the finger.

Skyped

All those concerts she never saw, that hand print spackled over with make-up, the halter tops he threw out with the leftover mashed potatoes and those dry veggie stars the cat wouldn't eat are in that smile, as she sits on the edge of the bed—five states between them—a naked stranger beside her waving, fish-eyed on the screen, toasting up a bottle of gin.

   "Hi Dad."

Book of Facts

As she hands him a beer and opens one for herself, she says, "Did you know, if you place a minute amount of liquor on a scorpion, it will instantly go mad and sting itself to death?"

He searches her eyes for clues. Does she know about him screwing around? Is that what this is about?

He shrugs.

"Well, it's true," she says. For several days now she's followed him about their small apartment, reading from a "book of facts." And for weeks before that, he'd find her crazy doodles, in smeared red ink, everywhere. One, he recalled, looked like a man hanging by his testicles. But she'd insisted it was a dog on a leash, admittedly abstract, with big, bulging eyes. And another of a man's head, eerily familiar, circled by a swarm of angry eyes, scribbled on the edge of a shopping list. She told him, and with a straight face, they were *fireflies*. That they were all just doodles. What'd he expect? They weren't going to wind up in the Louvre.

And now it was this, *Book of Facts*.

"Hey, here's one." She sits down at the kitchen table. Leaning against the fridge, he pulls his beer up, nearly empties it. She is still in her robe. He wonders what she does with her time, besides her artwork and torturing him with this cat-and-mouse. If she knows something, she should spill it.

"Lobsters," she reads. "*Do* feel pain when boiled alive. By soaking them in salt water before cooking, however, you can anesthetize them."

"If it were only that easy," he says.

"Huh?" She looks up, takes a sip.

"The salt," he says. He's feeling antsy. He finishes his beer and tosses the can in the trash. Wonders what Laura is up to—needs to get out and clear his head. "There's some stuff I've got to do," he says. He goes into their bedroom and grabs his jacket.

"Did you know Louis XIV owned 413 beds?" she calls out. "Now why would anyone need so many? You'd think one would be enough."

Christ! He shakes his head. "I know what you mean," he calls back. "Kings—go figure. Look, I've got to leave for a bit." He glances in the dresser mirror, slips into his jacket and combs his hair. "Some important documents I left at work. I've got a deadline." He heads back to the kitchen.

"What dead lions?" she says without looking up. She's bent over her outstretched arm on the table. He gazes at her pressing the red pen point against her forearm—sketching furiously, even grimacing once, as if she'd punctured the skin.

"*Deadline,*" he repeats, from where he's suddenly stopped—trying to make out the image.

She finishes her drawing and looks up—smiles. "Only kidding," she says, "I heard you the first time." It's a smile, after all these years, he hasn't seen before. But it slides away quickly, like ice down a windshield. He stares at her drawing, thinking—*it can't be!* That *can't* be what it looks like.

She stands then; holding out her arm—eye level. "Sure," she says, and her old smile is back. "But before you go, come over here and look at my new tattoo."

Uncle Sal

They were everywhere, anywhere my Aunt Rose couldn't find them. Those nudist magazines slid under old tires and boards. With names like: *Sun-Baked Babes, Strip & Dip*, and *Tan in the Sand*. Sun-bright women playing ping-pong and tug-of-war in the buff. My Uncle Sal digging them out of garage clutter; my young eyes bugging out as he slipped one under my shirt and patted it. The stink-eye my Aunt Rose gave back at the house—the runes she read as I stared down at my shoes; the cookies she gave me anyway—the daggers he got, heading for a six-pack to wash it all down.

King of Mastication

He curled over his last whiskey. It was nearly closing time and the old gal on the stool next to him leaned in, penetrating the invisible shield he thought surrounded him.

"I was on American Bandstand once," she said.

He turned and looked at her. It was like one of those 3-D movies where the sudden, exaggerated close up is jarring—the make-up piled on thick and too much enamel between those red lips to take in at close range.

She pointed at the TV above them in the corner. Glenn Ford was slow dancing with a pretty redhead.

"Made me think of it. The dancing. I could really hoof once."

"You mean Dick Clark?" he said.

"Now there's a name. *Dick*. Who'd want it?" She took her beer and emptied it. He thought she must have been a real looker once.

"Buy a girl a last one?"

"Sure," he said, waving the barkeep over and he gave her a fresh one.

"What do you do?" she asked.

"I'm retired," he said. "But I write a little."

"You're distinguished looking. I like that. Most guys in here dress like slobs. You writing a novel?"

He gazed in the mirror past the stacked bottles. His tie was on crooked. What was left of his hair was grey with bits of it standing straight up. The word "distinguished" bounced around in his head. Earlier that day he had lowered his wife of thirty-eight years in the ground. Tomorrow, he thought, he'd be one of those slobs.

"I'm writing a piece on Mr. Wrigley, called *The King of Mastication*".

She laughed and he noticed there was lipstick on her teeth.

"How many times a day do you have to do it to get a title like that?"

"*Mastication*," he corrected, "the gum guy. A biography."

"Un-huh," she said and winked—curled her hand around the bottle neck and moved it up and down.

"Last call," the bartender announced and he drained his whiskey, felt it burn its way down with the rest. He was done.

She toasted herself in the bar mirror and finished her beer, slid from the stool smoothing out her skirt. He imaged her young, spinning about on American Bandstand with the cameras on her, her hair bobbing, her dress a perfect circle.

She told him her name was Alice, but he wished she hadn't. Glenn Ford and the redhead turned into a little white dot in a black field, which lingered for a while in his vision. He stared up at it, absently straightening his tie till it was gone.

The Big Head and the Little Head

Ed is bench pressing his Great Dane out back. His girlfriend, Sandie, and I can see him through the sliding glass door. Occasionally, the animal looks at us with wide eyes, suspended over Ed's bulging chest.

Ed is an old friend who's been letting me stay at his place since Fran left me. I've returned the favor by banging his girlfriend. But in all fairness, Sandie hasn't made it easy to resist. And neither has Ed, with his passion for cage fighting and being at the gym 24/7, rolling around with other brutes while his girl and I are rolling around every which place. I feel like shit about it. Really. I remember this *Seinfeld* episode where Jerry explains how, with guys, it's the little head always telling the big head what to do. It's like that. I'm not saying it's right, or impossible to keep my distance. But close.

Sandie lets Thor in, as Ed pounds an old tractor tire with a sledge hammer. His shirt off and his muscle-strained body brings some of the tattoos on his arms and shoulders to life. Thor comes over and I pat his head. Equally unfaithful, he sometimes watches us in the act, peacefully licking his nuts when he should be growling.

Sandie sugars the French toast and her robe swings open. She smiles over before closing it and making a bow of her sash. I give a snowy piece to the dog and he swallows it whole, gazes up at me with one of those meaningful looks, wagging his tail.

Ed is out there doing pull-ups on a rusty bar which looks like it could snap at any moment. Sandie is singing as she puts another egg-soaked slice, sizzling into the pan. Sometimes, in life, things are just too damn easy for one's own good.

Freeway Jesus

When Joe saw Jesus lying in the middle of the road in His humble robes, he heard a shriek, not unlike that of a castrato or a startled banshee, and realized it was his own.

"Christ," Anne said, bracing herself as he veered around a colorfully thorned, blood-speckled head.

"I know," he said. In the last two months he'd run over a cat (mostly black) and more recently, a pigeon (which he didn't think was possible)—and now this.

He looked in his rearview mirror at the huge plaster of Paris lawn statue and shook his head. "It's a sign," he said. "And you can believe that."

"And what's it say, Joe?"

"I don't mean a sign, sign. I mean a *sign*. Biblical and shit."

"I get it. And what do you think it means?"

He tossed the joint they were sharing out the window along with the bottle of wine they were saving for later.

"Hey!"

"That thing was there for a reason."

"Yeah, because some numbnuts didn't tie it down properly and it dropped out the back of his pickup."

"Pretty shallow," he said.

"You're just loaded is all."

"Double pretty shallow," he said. "I don't need the sky to drop down on my head." He looked up beyond the clouds. "I get it," he said. "Things are gonna be different. Count on it."

"You mean *more boring than they already are* different?"

"Sure, joke."

But she wasn't. She opened the window, letting the

wind whip her hair. What if he'd seen a porta-potty spilled out on the highway, she thought. How might that change things?

She watched him move into the slow lane, stare out at the road intently, bent over the wheel like a little old man. She lit a cigarette and went through a list of possibles in her head. She was young and the list was long.

"Christ," she said.

"Damn straight," he told her. *"I know."*

Once I Was an Oyster

"I was an oyster once," my mother says, looking at my younger sister in her prom dress flared out in front of us like she pulled a ripcord, posing. My dad takes a picture with his Polaroid. The world has been sized down with that simple, instant gratification device of his and the loves that have passed through it. He pulls a wet newborn out and waves it into drying.

"Quit talkin' crazy," he says.

Once, my mother, when we were little, said we were having monkey for Thanksgiving. Said she was tired of "The Bird." That I could have one arm, though it might be a little furry, and Sister, the other. I pictured little grey hands and my father carving its torso. My sister, who always liked monkeys, including King Kong, started crying. Finally Mother said she was only kidding. That of course we were having turkey just like always. She handed her a hanky. "Now dry your tears, silly," she said.

My sister looks at her now adjusting her corsage, her date peering at the misty-eyed former oyster slumped on the couch.

"Huh?" my sister says.

"Yeah, for nine months I was an oyster. And you're the little pearl I made."

My sister beams and my father says, "All right, all right. Let's get another. You two by the fireplace this time. One. . . two. . . Say, cheese. . . burger with onions and fries on the side."

And before they knew what hit them, that familiar: *click-tear-wave.*

Body Art

I watched her twist her body on the sidewalk into a crazy version of the letter K, lie there still, her dress halfway up her thighs.

"Okay," she said and I took a blue chalk and drew a heavy outline around her. When the image was complete, she rose up and stepped out of it. "I saw you looking up my dress, you perv."

"Guilty as charged," I told her, lighting a cigarette, and she smiled.

"Okay," she said, gazing up at the building in front of us. "This one was a jumper."

All we needed, I thought, was the yellow police tape to complete the picture. What she was calling *art*.

"Give me a moment," she said. She closed her eyes and took in a few deep Buddha breaths, her belly rising slowly in and out. And I'd never seen her happier, since she started attending those *Be Here Now!* seminars. When she opened her eyes again, they were bright.

"All right, your turn." We walked up the street and I waited for her to select a spot. "Here," she said, pointing. And I lay down on my side, feeling foolish, but going along because it meant so much to her and it kept her off those meds that weren't doing a bit of good anyway.

"Lie flat," she instructed, "arms out. And ditch the cigarette."

Christ, the sacrifices, I thought. I took a puff and tossed the butt into the gutter.

At the lectures, some guy from India was telling them about the sanctity of *the moment*, to live life with the "Angel of Death" on their shoulder. That only when they confronted their own mortality—the fragile impermanence of existence, could they fully appreciate life. Soon after, she came up with this cockamamie idea with the chalk outlines, dragging me along.

"Now bend your leg. No, the other one. Like this." She pulled it back till I said, "Hey!"

"Hold still." She took out a big stick of purple chalk and traced a quick outline. When she was finished, I got up, careful not to step on it. We were at the end of the block and I took out another smoke.

"Last one," she said, staring down at it. "Humm. Gun shot," she decided, finally. She watched me light up, and I thought she was going to ask me for one. She'd been trying to quit for months. But she took out a pack of gum instead, rolled two pieces together and popped them in her mouth. "Umm," she said. "Never sweeter."

We stood there for a moment and gazed down at the long row of chalk corpses. Her jaw really working that gum.

"I'm starved," she said, "how about you?"

"I could stand a bite," I told her. She grabbed my hand and we headed for the diner down the street.

Crooners in the Web

The poet sat in front of the desk at the employment agency. He watched the man behind it shuffle through papers. Noticed on his tie there was a legion of golfers poised to swing.

"On your information form you list *Poet*," the man said.

"Yes. I was thinking I might find something related, part time. Say, sweeping zeros into freshly dug graves."

The man paged through a thick binder. "You any good at filing?"

"I could do impressions, stand up," the poet said. He held his hands chest high, to where they looked like they grew out of his armpits. "What's this?" he said.

The man looked up, shrugged.

"A T-Rex pantomiming a warm embrace."

"How about custodial? Can you handle a mop?"

"A flashlight's jewels are best displayed at night," the poet said.

"That wouldn't apply; it's a day job."

When the poet stared at the man blankly, the man took off his glasses and began nibbling on the end of its temple stem. "Let's move on," he said.

"I enjoy roughhousing with oblivion, if that helps," the poet added.

The man looked at his watch. "How about packaging? The pay's not half bad. It's a temp position, so it won't come with benefits. But I've got several openings listed."

"A moist magic fresh out of the can," said the poet. "That listed anywhere?"

There was a window a few feet away. The poet noticed a block of sunlight highlighting a few tiny golfers.

"Sometimes oven gloves are required to hold onto one's desires," the poet said.

The man cleared his throat and swung the binder shut. "When bear traps sing, it's usually with their mouths full," he said. "You think I like this crap? Don't mistake a fly, buzzing in a web, for a crooner. I was young once."

The poet straightened in his chair.

"There's a position over on Lincoln. Die cut operator. Stamping out cereal boxes. If you hurry, you can still make it." The man jotted down the address. They both stood and shook hands and when the poet turned, he could hear the man cracking his knuckles.

It was a long way to the elevator down.

Pet Psychic

They were watching a movie where giant spiders were taking over a small town. During the commercial she said, "I'm going to see a pet psychic. To contact Louie Louie."

Louie Louie was her dog for twelve years, predating him for most of them.

"Give me a break," he said.

"No, really, I'm set on doing it."

She had this look where the cement had already hardened. He turned back to the set—a woman was trapped in an enormous web, her arms extended cruciform as she struggled.

"You mean like *clairvoyance?*"

"Something like that."

"Wouldn't it be a lot cheaper to get another dog?"

"You don't get it; you never get it." She sipped from a glass of wine. He offered her what little was left of the joint he was smoking, but she waved him off. He took a couple of hits then put it out. He wanted to just savor the rush. See how the hell the townsfolk were going to get out of this mess.

"Babe," he said. "What if they're bullshitting you? Just telling you what you want to hear?"

"It doesn't work like that."

"How do you know?"

"How do you know *anything?*"

What he *did* know, was not to bite on that one.

Spiders big as RVs were tramping down the street, climbing up buildings—chomping their way through the populous. Too bad it wasn't New York, he thought; the Empire State Building blackened by spiders crawling up it would have been really something.

"She told me how it works, if you *care* to hear it."

"Of course I do." He turned and placed his hand on her knee.

"Well, it's got something to do with electromagnetic energy. It's in everything. She'd be tapping into it to contact Louie Louie. Even souls have it."

"O—kay," he said. "I suppose that could work." He conjured images of a table in a dark room with a recording of ubiquitous barking playing in the background.

The pot was really kicking in now and he didn't want to argue it further. She was primed. Another, more vulnerable expression framed her face. No less troubling, he thought.

"Well, maybe we could scrape a little off the vacation money," he offered.

"Really? You mean it?"

"Sure—maybe."

"It'd only be this one time. Well, two, three—tops. Wow." She emptied her glass. "Hey roll us a fat one. Hell, it's the weekend." And there was a look he could work with. He began separating out the seeds.

He figured, as one of the spiders climbed on top of a bus and started rocking it back and forth, that it might take flame throwers or humungous amounts of electricity to defeat them. But nothing less, he thought, as he placed the joint between her lips. He was certain of that.

Behemoths in the Basement

I'm standing at arm's length from the 50's set, holding the rabbit ears, just so. The only light, a TV light—flinging an icy cast to every corner. My grandfather sits before it on the edge of his seat. The picture bows, then zigzags sharp as teeth, as I search to calm it with coordinates.

"This way," he says, waving his wine bottle. "More. . ." And the picture stills, while I inch about—its fickle corners twitching. In a moment the commercials will end and the wrestlers will return. And my grandfather, a slight man, will inhabit their oily bulk. Squirm in his overstuffed chair with each half nelson and scissor lock. Their well-timed pratfalls, his answer to a quiet life.

"There!" he says, raising his hand like a traffic cop. "Don't move." And I freeze, peeking over the aerials, while the vertical hold plays tug-of-war with the ring ropes— skittish again and I circle the set—Haystacks Calhoun massive in the small bright square—undulating; one cheek north, the other south. My grandfather's opponents escaping into the curved screen's edges.

"Wait! Wait! There. That's it. Good, good. . ."

My grandfather expanding visibly in that testosterone-laden light. His behemoth's hand around the bottle while I poise statue-like, holding my breath.

Wild Life

When my grandfather got old and wine-soaked, his tongue loosened. "I used to be a lion tamer once," he said, taking a long strand of spaghetti from his plate and whipping the air till it broke and my grandmother yelled.

My cousins giggled, gazing at the sauce and specks of Parmesan, the worm of pasta curled up on the table.

"Are you a lion?" he asked me. I shook my head.

"You look like one," he said, drinking straight from the bottle. "I used to put my head in a lion's mouth without a scratch." He bent back his wrists, one atop the other and curled his fingers. "When I got through with it, it was purring like a kitten." As he reached for another spaghetti whip, I opened wide and ROARED. My cousins went ballistic.

His face changed. He wagged a wizened finger. "Okay, wise guy," he said. "Shut your trap and eat up before it gets cold."

Dark Dining

Always up for a new adventure, Sylvie said, "We're going and that's that." He tried to pump her for information. But she just said they were friends of a friend from work, this couple, and it was called *Dark Dining*. And he'd better hold onto his hat, 'cause it was going to be different.

There were six of them, not counting their hosts, and they were seated around a long, low table on cushions, led to it like the blind, the seating designed for mixing. It was the darkest room he'd ever been in. Somehow they'd managed to snuff out ever particle of light. He imagined duct tape around blackout curtains and along the cracks under the doors. A hand came up to his mouth.

"Try this," a woman's voice said, an inch from his ear. Her breath was warm and sweet. It was the redhead. He was sure of it.

"Wow," he said, tasting something entirely new to him. He tried to tease out the various spices. "Ummm. . ."

He heard Sylvie giggle from the other end of the table. It was her flirty laugh he hadn't heard in some time. The next dish was equally intriguing and served in the same manner—a glazed fish of some sort. Those fingers to his lips with something savory and exotic—her own lips to his ear saying, "Open up" or "Down the hatch." He even licked her fingers once as they lingered there.

She was the attractive woman, the host he'd met at the door. She had long red hair and a pair of night vision goggles atop her head, making her seem otherworldly. Her husband stood beside her donning the same equipment, greeting guests.

There was a lot of low chatter around the table and pleasurable sighs. She left for a time, leaving him with an alcoholic drink of some sort which went straight to his head and other places. After she returned, the chatter quieted. He thought he heard Sylvie whispering and then a slurping sound.

The redhead handed him another beverage and he drank it down without hesitation.

"I can't figure. . ." he began, but she put a finger to his lips. "Don't analyze," she said. She bent closer and her hair swung down across his face. He didn't bother to brush it away.

He heard her behind him fidgeting with something. Then she said, "Here," slipping the night vision goggles over his face.

"My God," he said. *"Fuck."* When he turned to look at her, she was naked and smiling down at him. She removed the goggles and there was that sweet breath again.

"Try this," she said and like a little bird, he opened his mouth.

Legs

I

Outside the open window, clotheslines web the fat backs of the tenements. My mother reels in the procession of our segmented forms dragged, frozen, over the sill: shirts with arms outstretched, as though pleading, my father's trousers taller than myself. Sheets like glaciers, pillow cases you can break. . .

"Close that window," my father complains. My mother turns up the radio, dances with his plaid shirt melting in her arms—takes his pant legs and bends them into a footless arabesque, as my mother and I cackle, and he, looking over his paper, shakes his head.

II

One of the highlights of my father's life, aside from his racing pigeons, his coin collection, his single near-perfect bowling game, was that he once dated a Radio City Music Hall *Rockette.*

"God, she could really kick 'em," he taunts, winking at me conspiratorially. And my mother implodes into her chores—scrubs harder, or folds soft cotton with the sure and steady precision of an origami artist.

III

The new house in Queens is slowly brought to life. From the second story, overlooking the garden, my mother has fashioned, a seed, a leaf at a time, she hovers precariously, cleaning windows, as I clutch her legs for ballast.

She stretches and leans, and I squeeze tighter, and

occasionally she grimaces back at the fleshy tourniquet I have become. A spray of Windex and glass between us. Thirty feet separating her from the mangled form I imagine on the cast iron lawn chairs below.

"It's stuck," she says, banging the frame with the heel of her palm, the window on her lap, pressing. "Hell," she says, "I asked your father to fix this. Get me a hammer," she mouths through the pane.

"Try harder," I bargain.

"Just get it!" she snaps, clutching whatever she can of the half-rotted wood. "It's by your father's *workbench*," she emphasizes, when she sees I won't let go. *"Hurry!"*

At a gallop, halfway down the stairs, I picture her twisted against the wrought iron with its rusty flowers surfacing through white paint.

When I return, I am again her anchor, the weighted essential joining her to this world. And for a moment I cannot hear her, can only see her lips moving—the hammer poised.

Then: *"Jesus*, you're cutting off the circulation to my legs."

IV

We are continually picking feathers from the wet cement that drift down from the small flurry of pigeons my father keeps in a coop over the garage. Their sparse snow is on the leaves, and now onto the gray surface we trowel smooth. It's been six years since illness emptied my mother from this house.

"Allergies," my father explains, apologizing for his new wife, two decades younger. The entire yard and garden, a moonscape.

As the concrete hardens, I inventory: There are three cats, twelve holes to China, innumerable toy soldiers, and now, as we scrape against the stone borders—the impudent resurrections of my mother's perennials, buried here.

He starts out politely, a symptom he is ill-at-ease, then warms. A harsh remark—his endearment.

"Hey, bonehead, you missed a spot,"—his young apprentice once again. The louder, more strident the words, the greater his gift.

His pretty wife smiling, her sinuses content. Ice cubes clinking in tall glasses. And now my father's love complete, as I wave him off—the roll of bills he pushes into my pocket.

"Here," he says. "Take it, or I'll break your legs."

Stuffed

We're old school, us clowns, folded up inside the gutted-out VW bug, just right. No trapdoor under the car, like some think, for an endless bunch of us to climb into a false bottom, then step out cool as hell one after another in unimaginable numbers—the kids squealing, their parents oohing and ahhing.

We're a puzzle of folded limbs and torsos we've perfected like they did building the pyramids. You couldn't slide a credit card between us.

"You cut a butt bomb, you're dead," Pete says.

"Likewise," Allen tells him. And it's all in good fun.

But not me and Mel. Not even close. I know he's been cozying up to Sheila lately, that trick-rider I've been seeing. He and me are pressed together like two jigsaw pieces and I'm digging an elbow into his ribs. I've got a few muscles under this get up and I'm giving it to him good. And he knows he's got it coming and doesn't cry out. You can almost see the blood rushing to his face under all that make-up.

"You get my drift?" I tell him.

"I can't breathe," he says.

"Good," I tell him, "remember the feeling."

He nods. "Okay," he whispers, straining to speak. I hope for his sake he means it.

A few of the fellas have already climbed out and things are loosening up. As each of us exits, the ringmaster counts into his mic with the audience counting along. It's nearly my turn and I give him one last poke for good measure and he groans.

"Sev-en!" I hear as I set foot in the ring with a goofy smile and waving my arms, despite the stiffness. The kids are so excited. It never gets old. The higher the number, the louder they get.

Sheila's up next and I see her in the wings. She gives me a wink. She's wearing that skimpy blue outfit I love. I shoot her a smile even bigger than the one that's painted on.

Family Secret

One night, when my father came home drunk after gambling away his paycheck, my mother (usually quiet as lint), said simply: *"You louse!"* and hit him over the head with a small hammer she grabbed from the utility drawer, while he stood there and took it.

When he finally sat on the sofa, dripping blood all over her plastic slipcovers, my mother put a hat on him and drove him to the hospital.

As a shaved patch and stitches suddenly appeared, we told everyone, even family, my father was mugged in the parking lot back of Stacey's, after picking up some aspirin for one of my mother's world famous migraines. "They got him from behind," we said. "Never knew what hit him." And nobody was the wiser, seeing as how sweet my mother always was.

When a detective came to the house with a small notebook and a big smile, my mother served him coffee in Grandmother's fancy china and a big plate of her Crunchy Nut Delights.

No perpetrators were ever found.

Jacked Up

They couldn't find scorpions, like in those Spaghetti Westerns, tied to either end of a table—their stingers ominously curled, so they used a couple of jacks rooted from the toy box in her son's room and placed them where a losing hand might fall, began arm wrestling. Needle-poked arms, one against the other.

She shook her head.

A biker rumbled by on his Harley and she imagined herself on back, arms around a thick waist going *anywhere*. Watching his collar flap like small wings. Plenty big enough.

She exhaled and smoke flattened against the glass. When she went over and scooped the jacks from the table, they both said, *"Hey!"*—still holding hands. She looked at them, her cigarette squinting one eye shut.

And somewhere was her man saying, "What the fuck?"

And somewhere was the TV going in the next room.

And somewhere was distance filing down the Harley into a little piece.

After the Earthquake

During the blackout we listen to news on my daughter's clown radio, tuning in disaster with a twist of a bulbous red nose.

•

Fearful the food will rot; we empty out the fridge and take it to the lawn, which night has erased. *Picnic*, my daughter says, giddy with play and innocence—the house of straw we exit, the big bad wolf could blow away at any moment.

•

Back inside, our child asleep on my lap. The clown radio on hers, empty now of news and spark. My wife asks if I'm still hungry. I shake my head. But it's dark. *What?* she says. *I'm good*, I tell her. Lighting another candle for the night to eat.

Accessories

There were thousands of woman's shoes scattered along the right lane of the highway. No truck overturned, no flares sparking against the road. Just the shoes and my wife yelling for me to pull over.

We'd just left the hospital for another round of chemo, and a minute earlier she was headed for the couch—a pile of magazines and a TV guide in the back. But now she had one hand on the door handle and her head out the window.

They looked high-end—a vast mishmash, flung here and there, and finding a pair that matched, and a pair that fit, seemed incredibly unlikely, and the last thing I wanted was to be rear-ended by some rubbernecker dazzled by the sight. But no matter—there she was out of the car among them, a little wobbly, but bent over like a happy farmer, forming the front of her housedress into a basket and filling it with careful selections. Running a hand over the colorful landscape. Registering a small flare of excitement as she pulled another from the clutter.

Then finally, her basket full, she slow-walked through the lumpy sprawl and stood in front of the car, unfurled her dress and let her catch fall. Trying them on, one by one, leaning against the hood—four pairs. Smiling, posing— brighter than I'd seen her in far too long, settling on the cherry-red pumps, a little loose, but what did that matter? They matched, so she'd already beaten the odds, and we drove off with them in her lap, not saying anything.

Hey, You're Not Harold!

Gil was driving down Clay, late, when he saw the naked woman lunge from a window.

"Christ!" He stopped suddenly a few cars up—pictured her cracked-open skull, and the blood. . . Jesus—he didn't want to see it.

He wanted to tear out of there, but it was a third floor window. You could survive a height like that. It'd mess you up pretty good, depending on how you landed, but you could survive it.

He wished he had a cell phone. Living alone, he'd never needed one. But now he'd give anything to be able to put in a call and be done with it.

His mind scrambled. Who was *he* to play God? Maybe she didn't want to be saved. Hadn't he considered cashing it in before? It passed. But perhaps it passed one too many times for this one. Then again—what if she fell? No, she jumped all right. No fancy swan dive, but no accident either. No sense kidding himself on that count. But still. . .

He leaned against the door with his hand on the handle; his knees banging back and forth. He had to do *something!* Perhaps CPR. They'd had someone at work show them how to do it on a dummy. But flesh and bone and blood—that was a different story. He looked around— the streets were empty. It was on *him*. No two ways about it. His heart hammered.

Hell, he almost wished she didn't make it. Then hated himself for thinking it. Imagined her lying there, groaning—*a last regret*.

"Damn!" He backed the car up. Got out and hurried toward the body—stopped as something landed, soundlessly at his feet.

Another and another glided down from the window. She was surrounded by a litter of colorful dresses. As he edged closer he saw her head—its silky tresses splayed against the walk. He picked it up. It stared back at him wide-eyed, with garish red lips coquettishly parted. The rest of the mannequin lay twisted at his feet.

Then a shrill woman's voice fell down from the third floor window as well.

"Is that you, you lying son of a bitch?" it said. "Here... here's your other friend."

He moved just in time, as the dress dummy crashed beside him. He looked up to see an attractive woman in a half-open robe leaning out the window.

"Hey, you're not Harold," she said. "Put that down, you sick bastard!"

He glanced at the mannequin head he was holding and dropped it. It rolled out into the street, rested against the curb. He turned to see a blue bolt of material tumble down, then another in a color he didn't recognize.

"You lousy creep!" she said, as he ambled back to the car, past that comely upturned face, gazing at the night sky—happy not to be Harold, whoever the hell that was.

One Better Than the Next

"Ooh, look at that one," my father says, with a child's wonder, pointing to a huge saguaro cactus, one among many (a desert full) as we drive to the red foothills of Sedona—three generations stuffed in my small Honda.

My 16-year-old ignores him, if he can hear him at all—the rap music he's listening to, tinny through headphones—a street litany accented by off-rhymes and obscenities.

"Your grandfather's talking to you," I say, nudging him.

"What?"

"You're grandfather's pointing out the cactuses," I say louder.

He looks out the window at the sparse terrain punctuated by the massive assemblage of prickly green arms poised skyward, shoots me a dirty look. "That's nice, Grandpa," he says.

In two years my father will be in a diaper, scraping his toothbrush across a carton of ice cream to brush his teeth (chocolate, not even vanilla). With the startled look of one who dwells in that netherworld where a newness glistens, blindingly, to all that was familiar.

They are moving in opposite directions—my son eager to be a man; my father quickly losing purchase, slipping back. There were always different coasts between them—the one cynical when the other filled with wonder. And now it reverses.

My son adjusts the headphones and shuts his eyes.

This is a last sweet time, crumbling fast. "Look at that one," I say, pointing, as we zip by.

"Yeah," my father says, his head half out the window like our old dog Baxter—the wind stealing away some of his breath. "One better than the next."

Hawaiian Shirt

The plumber eases out from the cabinet below the sink and asks for a rag. But as Margaret goes through a dusty bag in the basement, she is unexpectedly moved.

She pulls out Frankie's old pajamas, red rockets in a worn-thin outer space. And the yellow dress she wore in Greece—the geometry: *hers, its*—so different now. Followed by the ceaseless pull, pull, like a magician's scarf, of Laura's *Sleeping Beauty* bedsheets—faded with fairies and dreams.

And then she spots it, deep where it was buried—the bright plumerias, still in bloom: his Hawaiian shirt. The one he said made him look "Cheery"—so much younger. Like the Siren, eighteen years his junior, that would draw him to the rocks.

This shirt he wore when he hit her with the news, one hand in his pocket, jingling his keys as they walked. Waiting first for their youngest to leave for college, as though his escape were spring-loaded. The house, too big without them—pinballing through the rooms. Talking to the house plants, the walls—grateful that they didn't talk back.

Margaret pushes all but the shirt back into the bag. These are not fossils, she tells herself. This is not a record of my days. This is a bag of old rags.

It's hot and Margaret undoes the top two buttons of her blouse. "Here you go," she says, stooping to hand the plumber the shirt. He is a man in his forties with a wiry goatee and clear green eyes. Eyes that linger, Margaret notices, in her cleavage as she bends.

"You okay with me using this?" he asks.

"It's just a rag," she tells him. When he takes it, she fans herself. "This heat," she says. "How about a cold drink?"

"Sure," he says. "I've got some time." He smiles and wipes his hands. Capable hands, she thinks. And as he does, before she heads for the fridge, she watches, with a curious pleasure, the white plumerias blacken.

Measuring the Distance

My sister visits—her head ablaze with new drama. Her history is stunning. She has escaped the Moonies, a voodoo cult, survived a biker who chained her to the bed. And after each grand opera when, amazed, she finds the stage sets collapsed upon her, she visits.

Now, it's a defrocked priest who's left her. "I snipped the tips off all his rubbers," she says, as we're walking through the park a few blocks from my house. "I figured, why be subtle, right? I'm not getting any younger. I want to experience motherhood at least once before I kick."

I listen. I nod. It's what I do. I could be a parking meter or a can of peaches, it wouldn't matter. When we turn toward the baseball diamonds, I hear the *beeping*. See the blind players on the field, their heads tilted, listening for the *beep. . . beep. . . beep. . .*

I've seen this once before. A game of "beep-ball" played in the dark on a sunny day. And steer us toward it. We sit on a slope above the field and she doesn't miss a beat.

"And the son of a bitch took Sparky. You remember Sparky? That stray we took in. I told you about him over the phone."

"Sure," I say, but my head is in the game. A sighted pitcher slow-tosses the beeping ball to a blind batter. The batter listens, poised for that perfect moment when the sound is loudest. He swings, connects, a miracle of timing—a ground ball off the tip of the bat. It slow-rolls on the grass. The blind fielders, gauging its coordinates, tap the ground closing in, pushing through an erased world tarred black. Occasionally, I nod, say, "Wow," "Hmm," as my sister chatters on.

There are guide dogs on the sidelines, patient in their

harnesses—friends and family cheering as the ball is located, held up to the light. *The light.* I pull my cap down, shut my eyes. Hear *Shit head. . . Religious hang ups. . . Lousy lay. . .*

I imagine the sound of it, that beeping coming closer, in the dark, that black molasses to push through or drown in. Could I meet it, chest out, and connect as gloriously as they?

When I open my eyes again, everything is brighter, clearer. There's a wedge of sunlight on my sister's dress, highlighting a single rose.

"Look," I say, pointing. "The way the light. . ."

"The light—what light? You're not listening to a thing I'm saying," she accuses, then glances around as though suddenly snapped out of a trance. "And what's that God-awful beeping?" she says. "Huh? Can you answer me that?"

About the Author

Robert Scotellaro has published short fiction and poetry in numerous print and online journals and anthologies. He is the author of five literary chapbooks. His most recent collections are *Rhapsody of Fallen Objects* (Flutter Press 2010) and *The Night Sings A Cappella* (Big Table Press 2011). He is the recipient of *Zone 3's* Rainmaker Award in Poetry, and the author of three books for children. Born and raised in Manhattan, he currently lives in San Francisco with his wife and daughter.

9 781421 886503